Indulge

25 Indulgences to Unlock Your Sensual Self

Explore Your Erotic Nature

GWEN BUTLER

Indulge... 25 Indulgences:
Unlock Your Sensual Self, Explore Your Erotic Nature

© 2017 Gwen Butler

This book contains quotations from the following public figures and organizations: Mama Gena, Rupi Kaur, and Dr. Betty Dodson.

Published in Fort Pierce, Florida by Pipe Publishing, a division of the Stimuknowlogy Institute.

Indulge may be purchased in bulk for educational, business, fund-raising, or sales promotional use. For information please contact gwen@gwenbutler.com

ISBN: 978-0-9844475-6-5

Library of Congress Control Number: 2017958694

Cover and interior design: Stacey Grainger

Cover image by Rosendo: https://stock.adobe.com/46786667

Chapter image by Valeri Yakozoriz: https://stock.adobe.com/134886518

Page 100 image by Artemida-psy: https://stock.adobe.com/143651744

Contents

Foreword .... *viii*

Invitation .... *iX*

Shame on You! .... *xv*

Masturbation .... *xxiii*

Instructions .... *xxix*

Indulgences *1*

Chapter 1: Look and Map *3*

Chapter 2: Ready, Set, Jet *7*

Chapter 3: Got Panties? *11*

Chapter 4: Touch Me *15*

Chapter 5: Sex-Toy Retail Therapy *19*

Chapter 6: Workshop, anyone? *23*

Chapter 7: Climax Replay *27*

Chapter 8: 'Doin' It, and Doin' It, and Doin' It Well' *31*

Chapter 9: Sexy-Movie Time *35*

Chapter 10: Orgasmic Heights *39*

Chapter 11: Who's Your Daddy? 43

Chapter 12: Erotic Shower 47

Chapter 13: Talk Dirty to Me 51

Chapter 14: Go Commando! 57

Chapter 15: Smell Your Rose, Taste Your Cherry 61

Chapter 16: Finger-lickin' Good 65

Chapter 17: It's K-Time 69

Chapter 18: Mirror, Mirror, on the Floor 73

Chapter 19: Picasso, Picasso 77

Chapter 20: Dearest You 81

Chapter 21: Pretty Pajamas and Pearls 83

Chapter 22: Erotica for You 85

Chapter 23: 'Benwa' through Your Day 89

Chapter 24: Beyond Boudoir 93

Chapter 25: Guest of Honor 97

Resources 99

References 101

The Pussy Pledge

I pledge allegiance to my pussy
and to the Pleasure Revolution for which she stands,
8,000 nerve endings, designed by the Goddess,
one community, under the hood,
with pleasure and cliteracy for all

- Mama Gena

For all vagina-owners, identified as 'woman'
or not, of all backgrounds, orientations,
and faiths, and for their partners who share
intimately and genuinely with them.

To My Lover

In the mornings before I open my eyes,
in the space between awake and asleep
I think about you
... and your beautiful, powerful dick
I love your thrust, and the way you forcefully press into me
... and then I want your body...
I want to smell you, I want to taste you with my mouth
I want to cum for you
So I reach with my fingers, and I let my mind fantasize with you
... but it's only a momentary release until I see you again
My wetness is for you My Love
and I can't wait to have you again
I love you

-Anonymous

An Invitation

So, what is this all about really? I am glad you asked. Indulge is an invitation to intimately engage the most significant individual in your love life... You. After all, the most important and influential sexual relationship you will ever have is with yourself. Any sexual relationship, if it is going to thrive, depends largely on a few things: personal consent, mindfulness, awareness, intention, connection, engagement, touch, action, vulnerability and intimacy. It requires full engagement with no inhibition, and no fear. What better way to relate with yourself?

As a therapist, I have witnessed that individuals can love others only to the extent that they love themselves. Furthermore, our ability to connect with others is directly impacted by how connected we are with ourselves. Let me explain... if I am overly self-critical or self-judging, I will likely be overly critical and judgmental of others. If I am detached from my emotions because perhaps I learned this was the best way to deal with emotions, then I will likely be detached from the emotions of others. If I am sexually inhibited and/or sexually repressed... if I am not sexually liberated and empowered, I will inhibit my partner, I will repress their needs, and block the flow of sexual freedom and eroticism. This is not a malicious intentional action, it is often rooted in the unconscious. Sometimes it is rooted in oppressive upbringing or trauma.

Conversely, if I am patient and compassionate with myself, I will be patient and compassionate with others. If I am in touch with my feelings and conscious of their impact on me, I will be conscious and empathetic toward the feelings of others. And, if I am self-lovingly and sensually connected with my sexual needs and erotic desires, then I will be connected to my partner's eroticism and sexual needs as well. If I welcome the transcending power of orgasm and ecstasy at my own hands, then surely... I will welcome and desire the same in and from my partner.

The mindful and erotic sensual indulgences in this book are designed to connect you with your sensual, sexual, erotic self, which in turn will increase self-intimacy, self-connection, and self-love. And what of self-love? A sexually fulfilling experience begins with a personal love relationship with your sexual self first. Self love is the gateway to personal fulfillment... the place where when I am filled to the rim, not lacking in anything within, I can flow outwardly and genuinely to others. I can give of myself fully because I am enriched within. Self-love is sacred and not easily knocked down, it shields, protects and upholds. It makes you eat right, sleep right, work and function with integrity, it increases your empathy for yourself and others, and it reproduces... because self-love evokes creation, increase and overflow. Importantly, self-love grants full permission in the ecstasy of the eroticism.

You may have already indulged in some of these practices, some may be new to you. Either way, I encourage you to indulge in each one, at your pace, in your own time. Perhaps you want to invite a friend to join you in this endeavor, maybe a group of friends, or perhaps you wish to complete these alone. How ever you desire, I celebrate you for taking this exhilarating step toward sexual reflection and deeper self-love.

'Shame on You!'

This book is birthed out of years of what I call an 'un-shaming process'. I don't know your sexual journey and perhaps it is very different from mine. I grew up in a very loving, affectionate home where, although I could feel sexual tension and was exposed to sexual energy, I couldn't really grasp it. I didn't have the language, nor the permission to talk about it, much less explore it for myself. But I felt it in my body. Sadly, I remember being scolded and reprimanded for touching myself, and it left me confused. How is it possible that this amazing and wonderful sensation I feel when I touch this part of my body is wrong? Is my body bad? Has it betrayed me, and turned me into a bad little girl? Am I normal? Does anyone else feel this? And why am I getting in trouble for touching what's mine? Am I not supposed to touch myself? Is my vagina bad? Should I hide it? Should I resist and withhold this wonderful sensation... even from myself? This is how shame is introduced. And it is so insidious, communicated simply with a slap on the hand, a disapproving look or statement, and worse, a comment about 'dirtiness' or 'deviance'. I will not blame my parents for only teaching what they themselves were taught. This is a generational shaming, a curse on womanhood and our sexual freedom. It manifests early with potty training. Reflexively, 'boy' toddlers are taught how to grab the penis, aim the penis, and wiggle the penis clean above the toilet rim. There is permission; moreover, there is instruction and direction to touch their body. There is no shame, there is no place for it. 'Girl' toddlers on the other hand, are taught to 'sit appropriately above the toilet, use toilet tissue, wipe from front to back, don't touch it with your hands, and make sure you wash your hands clean.' What is the underlying message? It is dirty. It is a message ridden with shame.

This shaming is often sadly reinforced by the community through fear-laden, uneducated teachings, or no-teachings at all on sexuality - which has led to further confusion of the eroticism. I recommend a comprehensive teaching on the beauty of the body, sex, and sexuality for the purposes of procreation as well as recreation, and pleasure for both individual and partner pleasure.

I counseled a couple recently that had been married just under one year. She was 39 years old, and he 42. While they had engaged in self-pleasure through masturbation throughout their young-adulthood, they had never engaged in partner-sex. Society would call them 'virgins'. They came in looking for guidance and instructions on how to connect sexually with each other. We processed together, and realized that what they were really seeking was validation and personal permission to experience what their bodies were longing. They had finally received external permission (by way of being married), but were still being oppressed internally by years of 'don't even think about it', and 'don't touch it' lessons that came from home-upbringing and their individual communities. When we finally unveiled this revelation and reached this place of understanding, they were able to let go, start their own un-shaming process and begin their sensual, sexual, erotic journey together.

Sexuality is foundationally and fundamentally an essential part of our physical, emotional, psychological and spiritual lives; yet, we learn to hide from it, hide others from it, deny it, repress it, letting it out in secret spaces, only to feel shameful about it afterwards. It is sad and painful. A vicious cycle; and, if there is no immediate intervention, this shame grows, festers and develops into many sexual dysfunctions, deviant behaviors, and inhibitions that block the flow of self-love, and damages relationships.

I wrote this book because shame is and has been a frequent impediment to sexual health and pleasure. It is central to sexual dysfunction and dissatisfaction, and it shows up repeatedly in sessions with my clients. It is clear to me that personal sexual healing is imperative. A healthy sexual relationship is paramount, and it begins with you: the individual. On a more personal level, I write this book to share intimately with you a few ways to sexual freedom, through my own un-shaming indulgence process.

Ashamed No More.

"Masturbation is a meditation on self-love. So many of us are afflicted with self-loathing, bad body images, shame about our body functions, and confusion about sex and pleasure. I recommend an intense love affair with yourself"

-Betty Dodson, PhD

A few words on Masturbation

(Self-Pleasure, Self-Indulgence, Self-Love):

Masturbation is defined as erotic stimulation especially of one's own genital organs commonly resulting in orgasm and achieved by manual or other bodily contact exclusive of sexual intercourse, by instrumental manipulation, occasionally by sexual fantasies, or by various combinations of these agencies (Merriam Webster, 2016).

1. **Masturbation is self-empowering:** Whether you are with a partner or not, you are in charge and in control of your own orgasm. You own it. It is all yours. And the truth is, you cannot expect your partner to take you there if you have never been there yourself. Get yourself there, and then show them the way. Self-pleasure makes room for you to show up for yourself sexually. It prioritizes your sexual needs.

2. **Masturbation leads to a healthy mind and a happy mood:** Because of the increase in dopamine and oxytocin, which are all the 'feel good' neurochemicals produced in the brain, masturbation wards off depression and anxiety, and it promotes a happy mood.

3. **Masturbation needs no partner:** No partner, No worries... solo-sex is a wonderful thing! You don't have to worry about pleasing anyone but yourself, and you can be messy with it, silly with it, and you can take your time.

4. **Masturbation releases sexual tension, relieves stress, and helps you sleep better:** Feeling horny or stressful after a long day's work, need good sleep? Relieve yourself; after all, no one knows your body better than you.

5. **Masturbation promotes positive self body-image and sexual empowerment, and increases sexual comfortability:** It helps you become comfortable with your sexual body, your sexual sounds, and

increases your overall sexual body-image as you explore the wonderful things your body can do. Importantly, masturbation increases self-esteem, boosts body-image, and brings you closer in touch with your erotic nature. It also releases inhibitions and stimulates your sexual prowess, thereby reducing any residual stigma that might be holding you back. It is a mindful practice that brings you into oneness with yourself where you can truly be at peace and void of inner conflict. It is self-care and it is healing.

6. **Masturbation teaches you sexual tricks:** The more you explore your sexual self, the more you learn what your body can do. For example, masturbation can teach you

how to have multiple orgasms or experience vaginal ejaculation ('squirting'). You can discover new and different areas of erotic impact all over your body, in and around your vulva and your clitoris. You can practice new masturbatory techniques you may want to incorporate into your partner-sex life. Ultimately you become your own sexpert.

7. **Masturbation is SAFE SEX and it feels damn good!**

Instructions

In the following pages, you will be introduced to an **Indulgence** and the rationale for it, followed by a **Sexual Reflection**. Take the time the read the indulgence and consider how you might fulfill each one. You may modify them as you wish; however, please do not skimp on your happy endings. The indulgences are designed to push you to your edge, so I encourage you to lean into your discomfort and give them a try. For some of you, this pep talk is unnecessary... you may think some of the indulgences are 'vanilla' for your taste. 'Vanilla', meaning too light, a tad boring, or pretty basic. Please feel free to modify them as you wish, up the challenge. For others, you may be pushed to your own edge... loosen up and live a little.

If you are at all curious... Yes, I have indulged in each of these. They are tried, trusted, and true.

And now I invite you... to Indulge.

xxx

i like the way the stretch marks
on my thighs look human and
that we're so soft yet
rough and jungle wild
when we need to be
i love that about us
how capable we are of feeling
how unafraid we are of breaking
and tend to our wounds with grace
just being a woman
calling myself
a woman
makes me utterly whole
and complete

-Rupi Kaur, *Milk & Honey*

Indulgences

CHAPTER 1

Look & Map

Unless you live in a nudist colony, you spend most of your day clothed. Take those clothes off, and spend a little extra time in your beautiful nakedness. There is no greater feeling than walking around, sitting around, and lying around in the nude, even cooking in the nude can be fun.

Lovingly, look at yourself in the mirror and admire the curves and contours of your body shape. Instead of being critical and snarling at the things you don't like, take this opportunity to love all the alluring and sexy parts of you. Every time my best good girlfriend negatively talks about her body parts, I tell her 'Stop talking about my girlfriend's body like that!' We are worthy of love and affection with every inch of skin we exist in... starting with your own tender self-love and affection.

Body Mapping is a mindful-body navigation exercise I recommend to all my clients. It is a self body touching exercise designed to help you explore and discover your erogenous zones. Body mapping informs you on how you like to be touched and aroused.

Take some time to engage in Body-Mapping. Allow your fingers to discover, or re-discover your body. Love on it by exploring new erogenous zones throughout your entire body. Start at the top of your head. Gently caress your fingers along your hair, face and neck, tickle down the lines of your body. If you give your left nipple a pinch does it make the right nipple jealous? How does it feel when you run your palms down your bare hips? Caress your upper inner thighs with your fingers, tease your vulva a little, re-acquaint yourself... perhaps a pinch here or there, (or there). A little ice, a little lube... Go ahead... have fun with your naked self.

Rationale

Comfort in your nakedness promotes healthy sexuality and a positive sexual body-image.

SEXUAL REFLECTION: Indulge in your nakedness and tell yourself how good that was.

CHAPTER 2

Ready, Set, Jet

Agynecologist friend of mine tells me this great story of a patient in her 80's who came in for a routine check-up. All was well and her check-up was in good medical standing. At the end of her check-up as she was getting ready to leave, she turned and asked my friend, (her doctor) if it was safe to bathe in her Jacuzzi. Perplexed with the question, my friend answered, "Of course, it is totally safe to bathe in your Jacuzzi." The patient leaned in a little closer, and whispered, "It just feels so good down there, are you sure it's ok?" At this point, my friend realized what she was asking. She smiled, leaned in, and whispered, "Yes, it's totally safe to enjoy your Jacuzzi." The patient blushed as my friend escorted her out... and they smiled together.

Warm baths reduce high levels of anxiety and tension in the body and relax the mind. In a warm bath, you can also expect to be alleviated from any existing physical pain and inflammation. Jacuzzi baths are even better because of the forceful water from the jets and the whirling of the water on your naked body. Water flow is extremely sensuous and can bridge you to your erotic self.

Schedule some uninterrupted time to indulge in a warm Jacuzzi. Set the water temperature to your liking, play soft music or just listen to the water moving around you. Use bath salt or oils to hydrate your skin, and let the thoughts and cares of the world evaporate with the steam of the water. After you have relaxed (if you are soaking in a Jacuzzi or whirlpool), turn and angle your body so that you are receiving the water pressure on your vulva and clitoris. You can also do this with the running water pressure from the faucet (if you are not soaking in a Jacuzzi).

Did you know that the Clitoris's only function is sexual pleasure? Think about that... If that doesn't validate and prioritize female pleasure, I don't know what will! There are 8,000 sensitive nerve endings on your clitoris alone, double the amount that there are in a penis. In total, there are over 80,000 nerve endings in and around your vulva. That translates into at least 80,000 opportune moments for sensual pleasure using water-play. I say LET THAT WATER FLOW... and enjoy your water-play.

Rationale

Sexual freedom and creativity can be attained with whatever elements are within your reach. Water flow is extremely sensuous and can bridge you to your erotic self.

SEXUAL REFLECTION: Indulge in water play and tell yourself how good that was.

CHAPTER 3

Got Panties?

It might have started as a young girl with the matching wonder-woman 'underoos'. They made me feel invincible, powerful and strong when I wore them, as if I really had superpowers. On those days I remember feeling more confident and bold than other days.

It's no wonder I love bras... especially the sexy kind with lace, or a bold color, or print. And perhaps for obvious reasons, including and especially for my own pleasure, I always match my bra with my panties. It's a personal 'undercover pleasure' that always make me feel confident and sexy from the inside out.

Do this: For one week, intentionally wear sexy underwear. You can decide what 'sexy' means for you... it could mean leopard print, red hot, virgin white, or bubble-gum pink. No one has to know, unless of course, you want them to. Model your sexy underwear in the mirror, strut on your own runway, perhaps take a personal selfie as a 7-day sexy underwear challenge. Remember, this is for your personal pleasure.

I wonder how this might impact you throughout the day, as you move about, and then later as you return home. What kind of superpowers will it give you? I'm curious, are you?

Rationale

> **You are your greatest lover. Dressing for yourself is loving yourself.**

SEXUAL REFLECTION: Indulge in a week of sexy underwear and tell yourself how good that was.

CHAPTER 4

Touch Me

Touch is essential to human connection and communication, as oxygen is essential for breath. In a 2009 study, participants were able to communicate eight distinct emotions, i.e. anger, fear, disgust, love, gratitude, sympathy, happiness, and sadness, through touch alone (Hertenstein, 2011). It's a language all on its own.

Come with me a tad deeper here. Have you ever noticed yourself... giving yourself a hug, or rocking yourself to peace, or holding your own hands in support, holding your own head up, or easing the beat of your heart with the palm of your head? I can go on. If we pay close enough attention, we will notice that our own personal self-touch communicates its own messages and provides for our own internal needs. Go within and see for yourself.

I am sure you will agree, there is nothing more exhilarating and relaxing than the feeling you have after a really good full body massage, especially after a long week of work or an intense schedule of exercise classes. It is no surprise that the history of massage therapy dates back to a time in ancient cultures when it was believed to foster medical benefits and healing. A full body massage eases the mind, relaxes the body, and brings peace to your soul. It can also arouse your sexual energy. Just the thought of it now has me searching my schedule for my next available time slot.

Do this for yourself... schedule a full body massage. In full mindfulness and awareness (in other words, don't fall asleep), take the time to indulge in the touch of your body and pay attention to the motions of the touch. Notice the sensations you might be having inside your body as your therapist massages you. Inhale and take in the aroma of the essential oils, and notice the sound of your breathing in the rich sensual ambiance of a dimly-lit room. If you dare, also notice the breathing of your massage therapist as they synchronize their energy with yours. Commit to staying present with your body, almost as if each of your massaged body part is speaking to you. And in the end... when the massage therapist leaves the room, take a moment to touch and massage the areas they 'missed'... your nipples, your upper inner thighs, tickle your pubic hairs, massage your labia, your vulva... go ahead, let your fingers wander. But don't take too long, they're waiting for you in the hallway.

Rationale

Touch is critical for sensual self indulgence as water is critical for hydration.

SEXUAL REFLECTION: Indulge alone for a moment after your massage, and then tell yourself how good that was.

CHAPTER 5

Sex-Toy Retail Therapy

Gone are the days when visiting an adult toy store means driving through the back road of a desolate area to enter a frightening store that looks like it came out of a horror movie. Thanks to modern day sexual empowerment and liberation for female bodies, adult sex-toy shops have taken on a more sophisticated boutique look and feel. Even sexual toys have remarkably evolved into well-made, long-lasting, effective instruments of pleasure. In a well-stocked sex-toy boutique you will find all kinds of toys for all kinds of pleasure points, for solo and partner-sex. There are clitoral stimulators, g-spot stimulators, anal stimulators, nipple teasers, toys for bondage and kink play, toys made of silicone, stainless steel, acrylic, even glass. There are toys that are rechargeable, waterproof, water-resistant. And yes, there is a difference: water-resistant toys only 'resist' water and cannot be submerged (as in a tub), waterproof toys are impervious to water... these can be submerged (remember that). Sex-toy boutiques are also employed by trained folks who know their products and are able to educate, demonstrate, and match your desire and specific target areas with an efficient toy. Many of these fashionable sex-toy boutiques are also stocked with sex-educational books and videos, and sometimes they carry sexy lingerie.

When was the last time you indulged in some sex-toy retail therapy? Grab a friend, or go alone, and take a trip to your local (or not so local) adult sex-toy boutique. Go with the intention of spending time. Walk around, ask questions, pick up the toys, see how they feel in your hand, imagine how they might feel on your body.

Here is a good tip on determining which vibration might be best for your body: while in vibration, place the toy at the tip of your nose (which is a sensitive area; similar to the sensitive areas in and around your vulva). If you can tolerate it, you are likely to tolerate it in other places.

Importantly, a worthy toy is an investment. If you pay little, you may get a little less than what you expected. My advice... invest in a good toy that will last you and satisfy you for years to come, and make sure it is rechargeable. Go ahead, treat yourself... you have enough shoes, bags, and perfume. This one is a special gift. Enjoy!

Rationale

Sexual inhibition decreases with increased sexual exposure and education.

SEXUAL REFLECTION: Indulge in sex-toy retail therapy and tell yourself how good that was.

CHAPTER 6

Workshop, Anyone?

I am a real 'right brain learner'. I need visuals and colorful props, stories, and live interaction. It is no wonder that online classes never really worked for me. Even now, after years of schooling, when I am interested in learning something new I am quicker to sign up for a live class, seminar or workshop than pick up a book or study online. I like to raise my hand, participate, listen to other perspectives, and interact with the energy of my peers. This kind of setting makes my learning an enjoyable and indelible experience. If you're like me, this next indulgence might be perfect for you.

Sexuality education can come in many forms, and one of the more fun ways is through an interactive workshop. When you are learning a new sex-skill, it is always better to see it and visualize yourself doing it, rather than trying to picture it in your head (as from a book).

Many of the sex-toy boutiques, discussed in Indulgence #5, host erotic educational workshops taught by well-informed and skilled personnel. And, while learning from a book might be helpful for some, a demonstrative workshop might be more stimulating and informative for others. At erotic-educational workshops you might learn things like how to achieve orgasm(s), how to perform mind-blowing oral sex, or how to incorporate toys into your sex-play. Common titles and topics at a nearby boutique in my area include: *The Ultimate Orgasm*, *Dirty Talk and Role-play*, *Butt-sex Basics*. You get the point...

Get a group of friends together, or go with your partner. Make it a night out with dinner and drinks, or, if you wish... brave it alone. Locate a workshop and go learn something new to add to your sexual repertoire.

Rationale

Knowledge is power, and it's sexy.

SEXUAL REFLECTION: Attend an erotic workshop and tell yourself how good that was.

CHAPTER 7
Climax Replay

One of the most fascinating aspects of memory, is the ability to reminisce to the point of re-experience. If we focus deeply with intention, we can return to that place and time, almost as if we are really there all over again. And if we add the props, i.e. scents, music, or even return to the street corner or location, that memory becomes even more colorful and distinct. Think about it... the whiff of an old lover's cologne will summon old memory waves from deep within the brain, causing us to recollect some of the most endearing or erotic moments of our lifetime. Point in fact; olfactory senses are directly connected to the areas of the brain that are strongly implicated in emotion and memory.

In his book *The Erotic Mind*, Jack Morin says, "One of the most effective and enjoyable ways to unlock the mysteries of the eros is to reminisce about your most compelling turn-ons" (1996).

Take a moment to recall your most remarkable mind-blowing erotic experience. Was it the first time you had an orgasm, or your first taste of oral-sex? Maybe it was the first time you were fingered or kissed on the neck by a lover. Perhaps it was that time in the backseat of... or in the last row of the movie theater... you get where I'm going.

Indulge for a moment in that memory... what were you wearing, what was said to you, what did you say, what happened, how did you feel while it was happening, how did you feel after? No need to share, you won't get in trouble for reminiscing about your sensual sexual past. Just spend time... and smile to yourself, or tell a trusted friend. There is nothing wrong with re-living those mind-blowing experiences.

Rationale

A sexy memory recapitulated well can translate into repeated, more sophisticated erotic experiences.

SEXUAL REFLECTION: Indulge down memory lane and tell yourself how good that was.

CHAPTER 8

'Doin' It, and 'Doin' It, and 'Doin' It Well'

I was having a debate with a friend years ago about the impact of music. And while he disagreed my point that music impacted people's moods, I stayed steady on my perspective. How many times during a breakup, you play sad songs to cry it out? Or how about when you're really angry... do you turn up the volume to *'Can't tell me nothing'* to rile you up further? Tell me... what about when you're feeling especially in love with someone... is there an album or playlist that keeps you feeling gushy for them throughout your day? Maybe like me... you play salsa music when you're in a festive mood. Or when you're cooking... do you like to play soft jazz? Or Gospel on a Sunday morning?

Music is powerful and effective in setting the ambiance. Whatever the mood, music can usher in energy and escort the intended action. If you are a music lover like me, chances are you have tons of music in your library. It can be difficult to locate specific music if it's not organized to your moods.

If you have not done so, take the time to organize your music. Make playlists that match your common vibes. More specifically, create the playlists for your sensual and sexual moods. This will make it easy for you whenever the mood strikes and you want to add musical energy and influence to your flow. Marvin Gaye always gets my *'sexual healing'* just right for me.

W. H. Masters and V. E. Johnson, one of the pioneering teams in sex-research, designed a Four Stage Model of Sexual Response: (1) Excitement - initial arousal, (2) Plateau - full arousal, but not yet at orgasm, (3) Orgasm, (4) Resolution - after orgasm (Indiana University, 2017). Consider labeling your playlists strategically, and then perhaps ordering your songs according to this four stage model.

Here are some sexy playlist title suggestions to help you organize: 'iloveforeplay', ilovesweetsex', 'ilovetofuck', 'ichillaftersex', 'ilovetolounge', 'ilovesolosex' ithinkyougettheideanow... enjoy.

Rationale

Music connects your hearing to your sensations.

SEXUAL REFLECTION: Indulge in the sound of music for every mood, organize your music and easily access it when you need to. Tell yourself how good that was.

CHAPTER 9

Sexy Movie Time

I remember the first time I saw the movie Top Gun. I was definitely blown away by that passionate sex-scene... if you know what I mean! The way he grabbed her by the neck and had her against the wall... oh my! I can still hear the song in my head, *'Take my breath away'*. I was so aroused, and it was rated PG! It is an old movie at this point, but you get where I'm going... a good sex scene definitely makes a movie worth watching.

Can we take this a little further? How do you feel about porn? Let me just say this... I have found that porn can be useful to sexuality just as caffeine can be useful for staying alert – everything in moderation. I am picky and extremely selective when it comes to watching porn. Very personally, on the occasional solo-time when I want to indulge, I choose my own movie, to my own liking and I enjoy it... on my own. Now, if you are not into porn, it is totally OK. A 'sexy' movie does not have to mean 'porn'. You may have a favorite sexy movie that is not considered 'porn', yet 'sexy' nonetheless. It may have a few sexy scenes that take you there. Find yourself a sexy movie, make sure you have carved out ample uninterrupted time, cuddle up real cozy with yourself and indulge.

Important. A lot of mainstream porn is directed and produced specifically for the male-viewer. I have added a few websites that offer porn 'for the female viewer' in the resources section of this book.

Rationale

Visual scenes increase your ability to fantasize, and then reproduce your own scenes.

SEXUAL REFLECTION: Indulge in a sexy movie and tell yourself how good that was.

CHAPTER 10

Orgasmic Heights

You might be thinking, 'Wait a minute... have we not been talking about masturbation for most of the aforementioned indulgences?' Yes, you are right. What makes this one different? You know how it is when you try something new for the first time, and you like it! Like a new ice-cream shop, or a new favorite restaurant. It becomes so exciting, you just keep going back for more. It's the same with masturbation and new techniques.

In fact, learning a new sexual skill increases self-esteem, boosts body-image, and brings you closer in touch with your erotic nature. It also releases inhibitions and stimulates your sexual prowess, thereby reducing any residual stigma that might be holding you back.

Take your masturbation to the next level. Try a new position. For example, instead of lying on your back, why not straddle a vibrating toy on a pillow so that your hands are free? Or how about inserting a toy vaginally for g-spot stimulation, and using a vibrator for clitoral stimulation simultaneously – try to reach a g-spot and clitoral orgasm together? Use a new toy, or try pinching a nipple, lightly tap (or slap) the tip of your clitoris, near or on the hood. Practice 'edging'. This is when you are just about to reach orgasm and you gently slow down the process for increased and longer lasting teasing and pleasure. Or even better.. try to have multiple orgasms – just keep going after your first orgasm... don't stop. Perhaps, watch yourself while you achieve orgasm... use the mirror, make eye contact, watch how your body responds. Be creative here... go ahead and try something new.

Rationale

New masturbatory techniques bring you closer in touch with your erotic self as well as intensify your sex-play with your partner.

SEXUAL REFLECTION: Indulge in a new masturbatory technique and tell yourself how good that was.

CHAPTER 11

Who's your Daddy?

Imagine you have just received an erotic letter from your ultimate dream lover. I'll wait... let your fantasy flow here for a minute.

It is rather interesting where, and to whom your mind's desire will take you if you allow it. Your mind is the safest place to indulge in sexual fantasy... remember that. It is also the first step in actualization, in other words, if you can think it you can achieve it. So, when it comes to sexual inhibitions or deep desires unrealized, allowing your mind the space to fantasize opens the door to physical actualization.

... back to your ultimate dream lover. Create your fantasy with this person. Picture this person in your head. Imagine them looking at you, thinking about you, wanting you, desiring you. They can't wait to get their hands on you, and they have been thinking about you all day.

Imagine they begin to write an erotic letter to you. What would they say? What kinds of things will they want to do to you, and where? How do you imagine they want to please you? Will they talk to you throughout? Will they play a certain kind of music? What positions will they put you in sexually, erotically? And how ultimately will you cum? I'm excited just thinking about it. Have fun with this, take your time, and don't skimp on the details... after all, it is your very personal erotic fantasy. If you dare, write it, record it, or share it with a trusting friend or lover.

Rationale

Sexual fantasy awakens you to your erotic nature.

SEXUAL REFLECTION: Indulge in this fantasy erotic letter experience and tell yourself how good that was.

CHAPTER 12

Erotic Shower

The average person spends 8.2 minutes in the shower, according to a survey conducted by Unilever (Kinver, 2011). That gives us just enough time to wash thoroughly from head to toe without missing any body parts. I have personally noticed that the older we get, the shorter our showers are. And because they are so regimented, (step one - rinse the body, step two – lather the soap, step three – wash from neck, underarm, etc...), we don't pay conscious attention to what we are actually doing in the shower. Our minds are usually elsewhere; on our work day, or our to-do list, or that last discussion with the manicurist, etc.... we might even be caught up off-key in a song.

What if you slowed down just a little, and took some extra time to indulge? Take a mindful shower. Maybe dim the light in your bathroom, use scented candles, perhaps a little music if possible. Let the water flow down your body, watch the water as it travels over your body. Use the soap to softly caress your body, being mindful of the pleasure and erogenous zones of each body part. Softly pass over your neck, down to your nipples and belly button. If you can, remove the shower head and use it to target specific areas of your body, your neck and shoulders, your nipples, your inner thighs, your legs and butt, your vulva, your clitoris... use different speeds and intensities of the water pressure to your liking. Take your time, close your eyes, and enjoy your erotic shower.

For added pleasure, bring in a water-resistant sex toy or vibrator... your body will thank you, trust me.

Rationale

Erotic moments can happen anywhere if you pay attention. Slow down.

SEXUAL REFLECTION: Indulge in an erotic shower and tell yourself how good that was.

CHAPTER 13
Talk Dirty to Me

- 'I've been a bad girl, baby... I'm going to need you to lay it on me real good tonight'

- 'Can't wait to see you my love, I'm going to Cum all over you'

- 'I'm your nasty girl'

- 'You smell delicious... let me taste you'

- 'Mm, you like that?'

- 'My pussy is so wet for you baby... see what you did'

- 'Yeah... lick that for me'

- 'Finger-fuck me baby, I love when you do that'

- 'Ah YES!, pinch my nipple'

- 'I want you... right now'

- 'Come here..'

- 'Oooh baby, your dick feels so good inside me... don't stop'

- 'I like that'

- 'Deeper, yes.'

- 'I like that... YES'

- 'Baby, I'm about to cum!'

- 'Yes! Baby, Baby, BABY... I'M CUMMIN'! AHHHH!

- 'Oh my love, that was amazing'

See what I mean? Dirty talk is powerful, sexy, and purposeful. It arouses, affirms, provides direction, and intensifies your sexual experience. Here's the thing... you can't talk dirty if you are not accustomed to it. It's kind of like performing in a big on-stage play, but never rehearsing your lines. If you are not well rehearsed, it could come out all wrong; and, in these passionate moments, you want your stage-presence in place (script included).

Identify for yourself, the words, phrases, affirming sounds and sentences that most suit you, and start to practice them. Say them sensually to yourself, practice how you might use the intonations and inflections of your voice, move your body to the words, touch the body parts that you are referring to, close your eyes, or imagine yourself looking directly at your lover. There are a multitude of erogenous zones you could refer to... your neck, your breasts, your nipples, your thighs, keep going... I think you get the idea. Similar to the way you would prepare for your script in that on-stage play, prepare your dirty talk. Make it your own. If you speak another language, 'ay mi amor'! (Spanish, French, Italian, etc....), throw a few of those words or phrases in there for added sensuality. This is exciting! Go ahead... let loose and express yourself.

For added pleasure and indulgence, practice while using a sex-toy. This 'dress-rehearsal' will be especially effective if you are aroused.

Rationale

Learning a new sensual language makes you desirable and increases your ability to sexually communicate effectively.

SEXUAL REFLECTION: Indulge in some dirty talk and tell yourself how good that was.

CHAPTER 14

Go Commando!

It's not being 'fresh'... it's being FREE! Have you ever gone out to dinner, or work, or shopping with no undies? Totally commando? Ah... it is so freeing.

And before you turn your nose up, there is research to support that going commando can actually help prevent those uncomfortable vaginal infections. Because the vaginal area is already dark, moist and sometimes hairy, added covering will only encourage yeast and bacteria to breed and grow. There are other great reasons to Go Commando: It's comfortable, it's sexy, you won't have to worry about panty-lines, and you have fresh air flowing in and throughout your vaginal area. It's a win-win if you ask me!

Try it for yourself. If this is new to you, start sleeping without underwear. Transition slowly to going on a few outings commando style. See how you feel.

For added fun & pleasure, leave your bra at home too.

Rationale ————————————

> **Personal freedom leads to sexual freedom.**

SEXUAL REFLECTION: Indulge in a full commando experience and tell yourself how good that was.

CHAPTER 15

Smell Your Rose, Taste Your Cherry

Recently I was awaiting a friend in the lounge of a doctor's office. In the adjoining room was some of the medical staff discussing the idea of smelling and tasting their own vaginal fluids. I could not help but eavesdrop on the conversation. How I desperately wanted to jump in! There was debate back and forth, some expressing disgust while others expressed a hesitant willingness, and perhaps only one person admitting to doing so. I was fascinated at the different perspectives, and as a sex-educator and therapist I could not help but witness the embarrassment and shame around such an idea. Smell and taste my own vagina?

Well... why not? It is mine, isn't it?? Like smelling my own breath, or my own underarm, or my own feet, tasting my own blood, or swallowing my own saliva. I started to wonder how many women have never smelled or tasted their own vaginal fluids.

This may be a little out there for some of you, perhaps not so for others. BUT, if you have not indulged in the smell and taste of your own fluids, have at it. Take a whiff and see what you smell like, and then dip a finger and take a lick. Go ahead, see what you taste like. You may be surprised at what you discover.

Rationale

To taste and smell yourself leads to deeper acquaintance, self-awareness, connection, self-care, and self-love. This ultimately leads to complete openness with oral sex.

SEXUAL REFLECTION: Indulge in this smell and taste test, and tell yourself how good that was.

CHAPTER 16

Finger-lickin' Good

aph·ro·dis·i·ac
noun
a food, drink, or drug that stimulates sexual desire.

There is something incredibly sensual about handling, cracking, sucking, pulling out and dipping the meat of a crab leg that gets me completely aroused. I'm actually not surprised this experience would take me to such great lengths sexually, especially since my hands and mouth are really getting messy with it.

Originating from the name of the Greek Goddess Aphrodite, and since the 18th century it is believed that aphrodisiacs increase libido. Many of these delicacies common to us, such as oysters, clams, crab, watermelon and chocolate have been known to stimulate sexual desire. Now, whether this substance has an actual physiological impact or whether it is totally a placebo effect matters very little to me. Sexy and delicious finger-foods are always a great way to engage the sensual senses in a sexual way.

Go treat yourself to a nice spread of tasteful aphrodisiacs. Don't worry about your makeup or your lipstick. Use your hands and fingers, and get dippin'. Try it out for yourself. Get messy with it... and don't forget the butter. A foodgasmic experience for sure!

Rationale

Certain foods connect our sense of taste to our sensuality and eroticism.

SEXUAL REFLECTION: Indulge in that succulent meal, and tell yourself how good that was.

CHAPTER 17

It's K-Time!

Kegel exercises are a great way to strengthen your pelvic floor muscles. They are done easily by pulling in vaginally (as if you're holding in your urine) and then pushing out (as if you're urinating).

Having strong pelvic floor muscles is beneficial for many reasons unrelated to sex and sexuality, such as improving bladder & bowel control, and improving recovery from childbirth and other gynecological surgery.

Sexually speaking however, strong pelvic floor muscles can foster greater sensation during masturbation and partner sex, as well as intensify your orgasms. And since you need those muscles to push and pull, it also assists in vaginal ejaculations (or erotic squirting) if you're into that.

I personally have a daily reminder to practice my kegel exercises every morning at 10am. Do this: for the next week, schedule your K-time and Join Me! There are two sets of exercises I do: I pull in and out rapidly 50 times, and then I pull in slowly for 10 counts, and push out slowly for 10 counts. This helps to reach all the different parts of the pelvic floor muscular structure.

For added pleasure and sensation (whether solo or with partner), kegel during and throughout your sexual activity (especially during penetration)... roll your eyes back... nothing like it!

Contact a Pelvic Floor Physical Therapist if you are in need of more assistance with kegel exercises or pelvic floor therapy.

Rationale

A strong pelvic floor leads to sensational orgasmic experiences.

SEXUAL REFLECTION: Engage those muscles and tell yourself how good that was.

CHAPTER 18

Mirror, Mirror, on the Floor

There are so many different vulvas out there, all beautifully designed and uniquely shaped. Each vulva with their individual parts (mons pubis, clitoral hood, clitoris, labia, urethra opening, vagina, and anus) is expressed like artwork in different sizes, shapes, and colors. With approximately 80,000 nerve endings in total, you likely want to acquaint yourself with all the pleasure points within your vulva, not just with the touch of your fingers, but with a front seat viewing. You would be surprised at how many women have never fully looked at their own vulva and vaginal area. You might be one of them. No worries, this indulgence is a ticket to your personal front-row premiere!

The Mirror Technique below is designed to help you acquaint or reacquaint yourself with your vulva. This exercise is essential for sensual self-acquaintance and sexual confidence.

Place a sizable mirror on the floor and find a comfortable squat, OR, sit legs apart in front of a mirror so that you can get a full frontal view of your vulva. Every vulva is different, and your vulva is beautifully unique to you. Use your hands and fingers to explore your vulva and all of its parts. Spread the folds of your vulva, notice the different textures and colors. Notice the different sensations you feel as you touch each beautiful part. Lightly tap (or slap) the tip of your clitoris, near or on the hood. Take a look at your vaginal entrance, notice what happens to it as you kegel, or as you encircle it, or finger it. Use lubrication, or even better, allow your vulva permission to lubricate at your own touch. Let your fingers guide you. Take your time.

In the end, commit and become so familiar with the look and folds of your vulva that you can paint it from memory on a blank canvas. In fact, take a selfie of it in preparation for your next indulgence.

For your own sexual education, I have attached a diagram of the vulva and all of its parts in the resources section of this book.

Rationale

Know your body. Own your pleasure.

SEXUAL REFLECTION: Indulge in this mirror exercise and tell yourself how good that was.

CHAPTER 19

Picasso, Picasso

While on a retreat recently I took a glass mosaic art class. I went in with the intention of creating something from deep within me. As the glass pieces started coming together underneath my fingers... pink glass here, red glass here, orange glass there, I began to realize the formation of a beautiful and exotic vulva. It was the vision of my own vulva spread in a colorful mosaic masterpiece. I call it 'Labia Love' and it sparkles in my office.

For this sensual indulgence, I am summoning the erotic artist within you to an invitation of a self-portrait.

Go out and purchase a blank canvas, oil paint and some paintbrushes. With the memory of your 'Mirror Mirror on the Floor' experience (Indulgence #18), paint your beautiful vulva and be sure to include all of your luscious parts. If you don't remember exactly what it looks like, take another look, maybe take a selfie of it so you have it on your phone to refer to. And then, turn on your sexy playlist (Indulgence #8), pour yourself a glass of something, and Picasso away.

Camouflage your vulva in a bouquet of flowers, or a nature scene. Perhaps paint your vulva in different colors highlighting the most sensitive areas with brighter or deeper hues. Make it your own beautiful masterpiece and then hang that thing, and call it 'an original extraordinaire' because that is what you are.

If you are doing this activity with a group, consider hosting a paint party where each of you designs your own vulva.

Rationale

You are a beautiful masterpiece... can you see that?

SEXUAL REFLECTION: Indulge in your own erotic art and tell yourself how good that was.

CHAPTER 20

Dearest You

I love reading a sweet love letter, especially the romantic sexy kind. Write one to yourself.

Remember this is a 'love' letter. We spend way too much time being self-critical and not self-loving. Enough is enough! **NO NEGATIVE SELF-TALK ALLOWED!** This is your LOVE letter. Find yourself some beautiful stationery and list all the things you love about yourself. Tell yourself all the great things that make you the lovable human that you are.

List all the sexy and sensual parts of you, telling yourself how you love the erotic things your body can do. Be verbally and sensually affectionate with yourself.

For added fun, seal your love letter in an envelope, stamp and address it to yourself, and perhaps have it sent to yourself in 12 months' time.

Rationale

You are lovable and worthy of amazing self-love.

SEXUAL REFLECTION: Indulge in some good love-letter writing and tell yourself how good that was.

CHAPTER 21

Pretty Pajamas and Pearls

I loved to see Carrie Bradshaw in Sex and The City wear pearls to bed at night. Remember that? It was inspiring. It encouraged me to dress for bed in my own visual pleasure... perfume, pearls, and all. Too often the idea of dressing sexy for bed is intended for our partner's pleasure. And, while I do support that, I encourage you to do that for yourself. I am not necessarily talking about lingerie; although, if that is what you wish to wear... by all means indulge. I want you to be both comfort-able and sexy for your own personal pleasure.

Take a nice erotic shower (Indulge #12), and dress sexy for bed. Spray a little perfume, perhaps a soft shade of lipstick, put on a pretty pajama, a sweet gown or lingerie, or nothing at all (if you wish)... and don't forget the pearls!

Rest Well Beautiful!

Rationale

You are your greatest lover. Dressing for yourself is loving yourself.

SEXUAL REFLECTION: Wear your pretty paja-mas and pearls to bed and tell yourself how good that was.

CHAPTER 22

Erotica for You

Have you ever read erotica that completely turned you on? Exciting, huh? Have you ever read erotica that did not turn you on? What was missing? What would you change about it? Perhaps the sexual language, or the set up was not to your liking. Or, maybe it was too vanilla for your sexual taste. What if you could write your own erotica?

It is always intriguing where your mind's desire will take you, if you allow it. Your mind is the safest place to indulge in sexual fantasy. It is also the first step in actualization, in other words, if you can think it you can achieve it. So, when it comes to sexual inhibitions or deep desires unrealized, allowing your mind the space to fantasize opens the door to physical actualization.

For this sensual indulgence, you will be the author of your own erotica. Set up the whole scene. Where would it take place? With whom, and what kinds of kinky things would be happening? Consider your own fantasies, or perhaps your own erotic experiences, and use that content to set up the entire scene. Come on, don't be bashful; get all the erotic details in there. Make it last and don't skimp on the happy ending...

Later on, read your erotica aloud to yourself, maybe record it audibly for yourself (or your lover). Perhaps get together with your girlfriends for a 'night of erotica readings'. Go ahead... be the author of your own erotica. As an ongoing indulgence, consider starting a collection of your own writings... you never know where that can take you.

Rationale

Sexual fantasies can be fulfilled through your writing.

SEXUAL REFLECTION: Indulge in erotic writing and tell yourself how good that was.

CHAPTER 23

'Benwa' through Your Day

Benwa Balls are weighted marble-type balls, which are inserted into the vagina and used (with kegel exercises – Indulgence #17) to increase the strength of the pelvic floor muscles. They are also useful for sexual stimulation. Benwa Balls can be purchased at any adult sex-toy boutique.

I teach an evening class at a local university and on this particular evening I began my class as usual, sitting on the desk taking attendance and discussing the agenda for the evening. I'm a pretty animated lecturer, which means I often pace the room and use my body for added expression. As I started to pace the room I began to feel a tickling sensation on the inside of my vagina. It was rhythmic with the cadence of my pace, and might I add... quite arousing. And then I remembered... earlier that day while preparing for my lesson I inserted a couple of Benwa Balls to exercise my pelvic floor muscles. I completely forgot I had them in – Oh Shit! HA! No big deal... I just 'kept it moving', in more ways than one - if you know what I mean. The sensation of the moving balls inside of me throughout the evening was completely erotic and totally arousing. In all honestly, I was probably a little more animated than usual. It was my dirty little secret.

My advice to you... get yourself some benwa balls and 'benwa through your day'.

Rationale

> **Exercising your pelvic floor muscles can also be a pleasurable experience.**

SEXUAL REFLECTION: Indulge in the sensation of the Benwa Balls, and tell yourself how good that was.

CHAPTER 24
Beyond Boudoir

Not long ago, I got my hair braided in a thick, long-style Janet Jackson Poetic Justice Blond Beyoncé do-up. I was *'feeling myself, feeling myself, feeling my...'*. It was a fun and sexy way to exist in alter-ego status. My good girlfriend said, "You have to do a boudoir shoot!" Unabashedly, I said "YES, I MUST!" And so... I booked a photographer, set the date, got a sexy hotel room, got some wine, a sexy music playlist, and got to work! I think she wanted me in sexy negligee but by the time she had prepared the lighting and gotten the room ready, I was completely nude and ready to go! It was a safe space to push to my erotic exhibitionist edge. I was in the mood to be sensually and erotically expressive with my body, learning how to seductively arch my back with just the right amount of temptation, gently laying my fingers on my breasts and hips, gesturing with intention at the camera. Titillating and sexy... and awesome pictures to show for it.

Basking in your nakedness, (as discussed earlier in Indulgence #1) is a wonderful sensually liberating experience. Imagine being your sexy self in front of a camera. Come on, don't be shy... You Exhibitionist You! You know you want to flaunt your stuff! You only live once, and THIS indulgence, you MUST try. It is worth every snap of the camera.

Find a talented and respectable professional photographer and schedule your boudoir shoot. Think of yourself in alter-ego status, wear a sensual outfit, or go completely nude! Take photos and turn them into a nice book, or a calendar. This is a keeper for years to come. You in Centerfold! Make love to the camera, you know you want to... it's your ultimate 'selfie' time!

Rationale

Be celebrated in your nakedness and bask in your beautiful naked self. This is self-love.

SEXUAL REFLECTION: Indulge in a Beyond Boudoir nude shoot and tell yourself how good that was.

CHAPTER 25

Guest of Honor

Schedule a massage (Indulgence # 4) and then reserve a table at your favorite restaurant... for one... just for you. Be your own Guest of Honor as you wine and dine yourself. Treat yourself to a succulent meal, a glass of something delicious, and a mouthwatering dessert. Then take yourself home, and complete the date with an erotic bath (Indulgence #2), pretty pajamas and pearls (Indulgence #21), and a sexy movie (Indulge #9). Love on yourself, you Beautiful Queen.

For an even more adventurous time, plan a solo getaway, a spa weekend, or visit a new city.

Rationale

Self-care and indulgence intensifies self-love.

SEXUAL REFLECTION: Indulge as your own Guest of Honor and tell yourself how good that was.

Professionals I Know and Trust

Photographer:

Professional Boudoir Photographer:
Tmezz@bigeyephotograhy.com

Sex Therapists:

Gwen Butler, LCSW
www.gwenbutler.com
917-524-6797 (NY)

Nancy Owen, MA, LMHC
www.fiercewaterfall.com
425-223-7318 (Seattle, WA)

YY Wei, LCSW CAC III
www.colorado
relationshiptherapy.com
720-660-2321 (CO)

Lanie Hopping, MA, LPA
www.compasscaps.com
502-426-2777 (Louisville, KY)

Mary-Ellen Meltzer
781-255-8885 (Norwood, MA)

Porn Sites for Women Viewers:

Make Love Not Porn

Lucie Makes Porn

Lust Cinema

Lady Cheeky

Bright Desire

Sounds of Pleasure

Good Vibrations After Dark

Anatomy of Female Genital Organs:

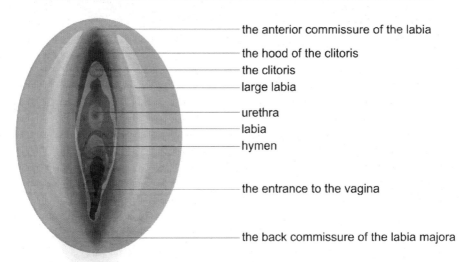

the anterior commissure of the labia

the hood of the clitoris

the clitoris

large labia

urethra

labia

hymen

the entrance to the vagina

the back commissure of the labia majora

References

Hertenstein, M. (2011). The handbook of touch: Neuroscience, behavioral, and health perspectives (1st ed.). New York, NY: Springer Publishing Company.

Indiana University. (2017). Masters and Johnson Collection. Retrieved from https://kinseyinstitute.org/collections/archival/masters-and-johnson.php.

Kinver, M. (2011). People's showering habits revealed in survey. BBC News: Science & Environment. Retrieved at http://www.bbc.com/news/science-environment-15836433.

Merriam-Webster (2016). The Merriam Webster dictionary. Martinsburg, WV: Merriam-Webster, Incorporated.

Morin, J. (1996). The erotic mind: Unlocking the inner sources of passion and fulfillment. *New York, NY: Harper Perennial.*

Rupi, K. (2015). Milk and honey. Kansas City, MO: Andrews McMeel Publishing, LLC.

Thomashauer, R. (2016). Pussy: A reclamation. Carlsbad, CA: Hay House.